Mary Seton

Part one

CW00853720

Introduction,

Some of these characters existed, but this is a work of fiction.

Mary Seton (1542 to 1615) was, alongside, Marys, Beaton, Fleming and Livingstone, one of the "Four Marys", Ladies in Waiting to Mary Queen of Scots between 1546 to 1568. Mary Seton served her Scottish queen, from the age of four, travelling with the young princess, to and learning the ways of, the French court where the Princess was destined to become Queen of France. Then accompanying her on their return to Scotland after the sudden death of her husband Francis the second in 1560, to become Queen of Scots. Remaining by her side through the years of turmoil which marked her reign, until her flight from Scotland and house arrest in Elizabethan England.

In 1585, after over thirty years of service to her Queen, Mary Seton retired to the Convent of Saint-Pierre in Rheims, where she lived as a nun until her death in 1615.

Some of the characters in our story existed, but this is a work of fiction.

It is June 1567 and Mary, Queen of Scots, is queen in name only, forced to marry her third husband, James Hepburn 4th Earl of Bothwell after her second husband, Lord Darnley Stuart, was allegedly murdered by a group of Scottish Lords. Queen Mary lives in fear for her life and for the life of her infant son, James.

She has appealed for help to her cousin in England, Elizabeth Tudor. But the appeal has fallen on deaf ears.

Desperate, she feels her final option is to get a message to her former brother-in-law, King Charles the ninth of France, requesting armed support or assistance with an escape to a French exile.

Spies for Bothwell watch her every move and she knows that there is only one person she can truly trust. Her only remaining, Lady in Waiting, Mary Seton.

In France, the "Armed Peace" of the wars of religion between the Huguenots and the Catholics is barely holding. Charles IX is trying to reastablish the authority of his crown, France is volatile, with another war close.

Holyrood, Edinburgh 1567

Mary Seton stood quietly, waiting to be summoned, the summer sunshine on her face was a welcome relief to the tension she felt in the pit of her stomach. Her servant, John Dumfries, paced impatiently. Causing her temper to become frayed.

"John, stand still!"

Dumfries, stopped and turned towards his mistress, moving closer to her and after looking around them, spoke quietly.

"I can't Madame, you know I don't trust these people, these..." pausing, his voice barely a whisper.

"Bothwell has his eyes and ears everywhere, how do we know this isn't some sort of trick."

Mary adjusted her bonnet, pushing her dark hair underneath, it was warm, and she longed to remove it, her heavy white woollen tunic was causing her body to sweat and itch, her long ankle length red skirt felt heavy. Despite her discomfort, she knew her duty and would wait.

She tugged on the arm of Dumfries, as she gently moved them both into the shade of the Gatehouse of Holyrood, The palace, once her home, now a building of fear and danger for her. Dumfries nervously flexed his fingers over the hilt of the dagger he always carried at his side. Mary looked at him, tall and thin, dressed, as always in black tights, britches, cloak and tunic, his white shirt collar standing out against his drab attire. His simple taste in fashion gave him the air of a reformer, a protestant. Mary was never sure with him. Religion, it was killing thousands in France, destroying friendships, families across Edinburgh and the rest of the country. Her train of thought was interrupted by a welcome voice calling out in French.

"Mary, Tu es venu (you came)."

She turned and threw herself at the feet of her queen, Mary queen of Scots. The queen reached out her hand for her to kiss which she gratefully accepted with both her hands. The two ladies, both raised in France, conversed as such.

As she stood Mary asked, "My queen, how are you?" She looked at her queen, her dress of black, a veil hiding her beautiful face, her auburn hair hidden underneath a dark hat. Lifting her veil, she looked thin, her face and eyes lacking their usual radiance, the dark colours she wore, did not suit her, she was always so colourful in her fashion and to see her dressed so solemnly was almost hurtful.

"Madame, my queen. If I may be so bold, you look as if you are in mourning," she tried to smile, "you are a new bride."

The queen looked at her servant, her friend. She smiled briefly.

"I am in mourning for my son, James. I am not allowed to have him here with me or even to journey to Stirling see him. He feels so close to me yet he is leagues away"

Mary stared her in the eye,

"This is monstrous evil madame, is this Bothwell's doing Madame?"

The queen lowered her gaze, and whispered so quietly, Mary had to lean in to hear.

"I have nothing to say about my husband" pausing and looking at Mary," and neither should you."

Mary bowed her head,

"I am sorry Madame; we have known each other since we were children and there are times, I forget my place."

The queen looked at her and placed a gloved hand upon her cheek.

"You are of course forgiven my friend." The queen looked over her shoulder and speaking now in English. "Mr Dumfries, please leave us, I wish to speak to your mistress alone." Dumfries bowed and walked out from the gate tower, into the Palace courtyard, looking up he saw a figure at a window, upon meeting his gaze, it melted away, out of sight.

The queen took Marys' hands in hers, Mary felt something small and thin in her palm. She took it, holding it tight. The queen looked deep into her eyes.

"I need your help, Mary."

"Anything my queen." The queen breathed heavily and smiled a little.

"I am being watched all the time, I need to flee, I need to escape, the Scottish Lords are against me."

Mary bit her lip in an attempt to restrain herself, but simply found she could not help herself,

"Madame, I may be speaking out of my station but even if this is so, the people know you are the rightful monarch, the heir of King James and a daughter of Guise."

The queen looked away again, parting hands with Mary, spitting her words.

"The people are under the influence of Knox! his pulpit and their non-papal religion. Scotland is beginning a war with itself," The queen paused, her gaze downward, contempt in her voice and words, "because of men such as him."

Mary, in an attempt to reassure her Queen, and herself. "Madame, do not fear Knox, he is nothing more than a," she paused considering her words, "a common rabble rouser."

The Queen, raising herself to her full height, her hazel brown eyes locking onto Marys. "He has the hearts, minds and the ear of the common rabble, and that is what makes him so dangerous."

Mary clutched the item in her palm, she dared not look at it, for fear of prying eyes. It felt like a letter, a message. She breathed deeply and whispered,

"Madame, is this a letter, if so, who is it for?"

"The Duke of Rouen, do you remember him, he was there when I married my beloved Francis he is," she paused tears forming in her eyes, "was, one of our closest friends, take this letter to Rouen for him, for me Mary, he can give to my brother in law, Charles, he can send troops or at least a ship, to rescue me from this prison that my husband has constructed for me, please Mary, I can trust no-one else."

Mary thought for a moment,

"Of course, my queen, consider it done."

The queen squeezed her hands, placing a gift into them, later, when Mary dared to look, she saw her Queens very own rosary beads.

"You must go, if I am out of sight for too long, they become suspicious, go, God speed, I will pray for your safety." The queen released her hands and walked away, as Mary curtsied and dropped her gaze. Once her queens' footsteps were from her, she rose herself and tucking the letter inside her tunic. She left the gatehouse, she walked over to Dumfries, he nodded as she approached.

"Madame, am I allowed to enquire." Mary stopped him mid-sentence,

"Not here, come we are to return home, we have things to prepare."

With that they walked out of the palace gates, John nodding to the guards, who fell silent as they approached, eyeing them with suspicion. Mary, with John maintaining his place a few steps behind her, started walking quickly through the Cannongate slums up the gentle slope of the Royal mile in silence. Where they continued, maintaining a silence until turning off the mile, entering the entrance to their street and home.

Once home, John and Mary both ducked under the doorway to enter the house as Mary was as tall as any man.

"Janet, Janet Spittell," she shouted then turning to John, "where is that girl?"

A small girl of teenage years, dressed in a one piece plain brown servants' dress with no tunic or fine trimmings, only a white apron, reaching down to her ankles. She lifted it slightly as she came running from the scullery where she had been cleaning. She stopped short of them, letting her dress drop, she tried to tidy her dark hair away from sight under a headscarf, which was speckled in dust, her pretty face was smudged with soot from the fireplace, her green eyes lit up at the sight of her mistress return. She smiled, her thin lips opening slightly to reveal a broken toothed smile as she curtsied.

"Yes madame."

Mary stood looking at her, then she turned to John,

"My servants, my friends, I need your help, today and," she paused, looking John in the eye, "John, I need your blade, your protection, I have to travel, overseas, for some time, I request your aide." she locked her eyes onto his.

"Madame, of course you shall have it, but why are we to leave? If I am to travel, I would like to request a reason Madame."

Mary held his gaze, John was unsure, but felt she was tearful. Mary reached out and took John's hand.

"My friend, I cannot say, not at this moment, but please trust me." she lowered her head as her voice grew weak. "Please John, do as I ask, if I tell you, I know I will be putting you and Janet in danger." John moved his face to hers, smiling.

"By travelling with you, is it not the case I am placing myself in danger, Madame?" He spoke, his voice a whisper, Janet, knowing her place, backed away from them.

"Is this to do with your meeting with," he stopped, and looked towards Janet, who, reading an instruction in his stern face, departed back into the scullery.

"The lady." he whispered.

Mary nodded, and handing him a purse of coins, "we have to travel as soon as possible, tonight or at the earliest tide tomorrow." Raising her head slightly to match his height, whispered.

"Can you go down to Leith docks and find us a ship heading for France."

John looked surprise.

"Tonight?"

"Yes John," she spoke firmly, "first possible sailing, Northern France."

Lieth

John pulled his black hood over his head and wrapped his waist length cloak around himself, conscious that this may look suspicious, as the day was dry and the air warm. He buried his worry under the thought of Bothwell's' eyes, he knew they were everywhere. If his mistress was planning a quick escape to France, then either the Queen, or Bothwell were behind it.

Keeping his gaze downward, he left the arched entrance leading out into the street, and hurried down to Holyrood, trying to pass unnoticed as the crowds of tradesmen, vendors shouting for sales, beggars, with grubby hands extended out, hoping for a coin or two to be placed in them, these were the people who criss-crossed the mile every day. Circling around him, swooping near him, like a never-ending river of people and animals. Avoiding looking up, for fear his eyes should meet, and recognise someone, he became just another face, albeit a hooded face, in the crowd. And avoiding the dreaded call of Giardiello, knowing the mile as he did, he knew what was next, a full bucket of toilet water splashing down from one of the wooden houses, walls painted white, the wooden cross beams black.. What fell, would lie in the gutter alongside the offal until the rain washed it all away

He stood near Holyrood palace and just for a second wondered if her majesty was watching from within, then thinking of Bothwell's eyes, he hurried North towards Leith and the docks. He smelt the harbour before he saw it.

He hated the sea, always had, as a young boy he had watched as his dear father had left for the sea, never to return, leaving him and his mother in poverty, and, although this was only a harbour, it reminded him of what the sea would take, then never give back. As he approached the water edge, he heard the noises of the harbour, the yelling of the fishermen, the creaking of the ropes as they strained to keep the boats moored in place, and the dull thud of those boats as they knocked into each other as the harbour swell raised and lowered them.

He lowered the hood of his cloak, covering his eyes and entered the harbour office, little more than a poor old rotten wooden hut near the small jetty which led out to the larger boats. He stopped, allowing his eyes to became accustomed to the poor lighting provided by what little daylight could fight its way past the dirt on the small grimy window.

Behind a tall, roughly constructed counter, stood a large unshaven man in an aged, dirty leather apron. Hanging from his shoulders, it stretched and strained itself across his belly, down to his bare blackened feet, underneath, he wore a grubby shirt. He sat and drank deeply from a cracked pewter tankard; he wiped his large round face with his stained sleeve as his small dark eyes spied John. Looking John up and down he spoke slowly, his Leith accent recognisable.

"Come in sir, don't be shy," this comment made him laugh loud, his mouth agape, showing his few remaining broken teeth. His fat chins wobbling. John, oblivious to the humour, entered, closing the door behind him.

"Good day good sir." John began, before the man interrupted.

"Good sir, am I, it would seem the gentleman does not know me." he laughed, but this time he looked over to a corner of the room, John followed his gaze, a shape, a person, appeared to be there. John felt unease, but, as he had business here, he moved towards the desk.

"Good," he stopped mid-sentence, his gaze following over to the darkened corner, a figure sat in the pale light. The glow of a pipe was all John could make out for certain. John paused then turned back to the man behind the desk. "Morning, my friend, I seek passage on the first ship heading to France, do you know of any captain who I might discuss this matter with?"

The man leaned over his counter, fixing his dark eyes on John. "Why would a gentleman, such as you require such a voyage?"

Johns' hand moved into the side of his breeches, feeling for the hilt of his dagger.

"That business sir, is my business, can you assist, or no?" The large man leaned back into his chair his hand rubbed his stubbled chin, then ran it over his bald head.

"Perhaps I can," he smiled his toothless smile, "why would I want to help?" One large dirty hand fell from his scalp to lie open, hanging over the edge of the desk. John smirked, releasing his dagger he withdrew a coin from the small bag of coins tied to his belt and placed it into the large flat hand, from the corner of his eye he spied movement, he quickly placed his hand back onto his dagger hilt.

The large man closed his hand around the coin and soon both disappeared under the desk.

"Go to the end of the North pier, where the larger ships are, there's a French ship moored there, The Dauphine, I believe is her name, arrived from Roscoff a few days ago, a trader ship. Ask for the Captain, he speaks English, seems a good man, he may help, for a fee of course." the figure from the shadows drew closer to John.

"Of course, I thank you for your help, good day." John turned to the figure, who was now close enough for John to see. That he was a small, slight man with a large strong smell. "And to your assistant sir, good day to you too."

"I am no-mans," He paused, John felt this was for effect, then he sneered the word "assistant. I am Charles Martell, perhaps you have heard of my family?" the voice was slightly refined, almost educated, his black tunic, leggings and boots looked well-made and clean. He spoke with what was definitely not a typical harbour voice.

"Forgive me sir for the slight, I meant no offence. But your name is not known to me, an Edinburgh name?" The man moved into view, removing his pipe, he was fair headed, with cold blue eyes, a hooked nose above thin lips and a pointed chin covered in a short, goat style blonde beard. In his hands he toyed with a wide brimmed, feathered grey coloured hat.

"No offence taken," Martell paused, "John, but I wonder why the good lady Setons' man servant is in such a rush to depart to France?" John physically felt sick at the realisation that a cold Bothwell eye could be fixed upon him, so soon after their Holyrood engagement. Trying to maintain a calm countenance, he smiled to him, gently nodding, as a form of greeting.

"Stranger, I know not of what you speak, I am merely arranging travel for a friend, now please excuse me, I am busy." He turned to leave but a gloved hand was placed on his arm.

"I am not so busy sir," John noticed the stranger looking towards the large man behind the counter, who appeared to be fishing for something under his counter, perhaps looking for a weapon? He continued, "that I cannot wait for an answer, so, if you would be so kind as to provide an answer, why the rush for France?" John turned and stared into cold blue eyes.

"The answer is my business sir, none of yours, now sir, if you would kindly unhand me," he gently took hold of the strangers' wrist in his hand and removed it from his arm, "I'm sure the Earl Bothwell has work for you to do."

The stranger took a step back from John, smiling to himself, "As you wish Mister Dunfries." bowing to John he placed his hat on his head, placed his pipe into his mouth and returned to his darkened corner.

John left as calmly as his nerves would allow, walking towards the north pier, his hand upon his dagger, glancing quickly over his shoulder, listening intently to hear, amongst the harbour noise, for any following footsteps. He approached the ship, La Dauphine, the prince. A cargo ship, small with the paint, once bright and decorative. Now, faded and peeling on its stern, ornate woodwork beaten to plain by years of sea. "Good, a simple working boat, anonymous to all who may see her," he thought, John called out for an English speaker. He was met with a quick response.

"How may I help you sir?" an old face with an accented voice appeared from above the deck. John looked at the man. He nervously stepped up the gang plank and onto the creaking deck. Making his way slowly towards the man, looking around as other sailors watched the sombre dressed stranger. The crewmen joking amongst themselves in French. John could only nod a greeting and spoke softly to the captain, his voice nearing a whisper.

"I seek passage to France for myself and a friend; you are returning there on the tide I believe?"

The man smiled, "That is true sir, please welcome aboard," he smiled, "If you wish to do business in private sir, the captain is in his cabin, please follow me." The man glanced at the group of men working around him, watching. John followed as instructed, trying to count the number of the group, trying to see if any were familiar.

Soon, with business concluded with the captain, which, as the large man in the office predicted included the passing over of coins. John stood on the deck, counting, unsure of numbers there. He shook hands with the captain, he quickly exited the craft and soon left the harbour. Walking briskly, his hood raised once more, not wishing to be seen to run, for fear that it would attract attention from, who knew? The man from the harbour office. Martell? John racked his memory, he did not know him, could not recall ever meeting him, did not recognise the name. Who was he? Another of Bothwell's spies?

And the sailors? How many were there as he boarded, how many as he left, the same number? Perhaps, perhaps not he was unsure, he tried to clear his mind, one could have left for another part of the ship, or elsewhere?

John chewed this over and over in his mind until he arrived home. Entering the house and calling out for Janet, the maid appearing in the small hallway at the sound of his voice.

"Yes John,"

"Where is madame?"

"Upstairs sir, packing her travel chest, she did not ask me to do it for her or ask for no help when I offered." Whispering to John, "what is happening?"

John lowered his face, then turned to her, noting the worry in it, he whispered.

"I do not know," he looked up the stairs, "I simply do not know, but we simply must obey our madams wishes." Julie nodded, then turned from him. John climbed the small, narrow staircase and found Mary in her room, her travel chest open, as she laid clothes into its empty mouth.

"Madame,"

Mary looked up,

"Do you have transport?" she asked eagerly.

"Yes madame, as instructed, we can leave today, at the gun, on a French ship bound for Roscoff, a port I believe you know, passage is on a small, old cargo boat. It has a few cabins, but that also means few other passengers,"

After hearing the name of Roscoff, Mary smiled, John did not, "Madame, there may still be a problem madame. There will be" He paused, "other passengers on his ship, others no matter how few, we are only two."

Mary stopped from folding clothes and looked John directly.

"I am not entirely sure madame, but a," he paused to consider his next word, "gentleman, well dressed and well spoken, it is rare for men such as this to be in the Lieth harbour office, or in any other sort of harbour."

Mary looked directly at him, "And yet you yourself," she gestured her hand towards John. "Well dressed and well spoken, were there?"

John looked at the floor, "Madame, please considering the type who are normally there."

Mary smiled briefly, "Please forgive me my friend, tell me more of this man, a Bothwell man, awaiting me, us?"

John continued, "I simply do not know, he was someone I did not recognise, or recall in any capacity. Though, he appeared to know me and seemed highly interested in my, our business madame, also, he asked about you by name."

"Then he is definitely a Bothwell eye? Mary sighed, "Are they one step ahead of us? Is this a trap?"

Silence fell between them as they both considered, until,

"Madame, I must insist on knowing," John spoke with authority, almost shouting, Mary raised her hand to silence him, then gestured towards the door to indicate that Janet may be listening. He lowered his head, John moved to enter the room, his foot hovering over the entrance unsure if it was correct to enter. Mary flashed him a look of impatience as she gestured towards the chair. "My apologies madame." He said entering and closing the chamber door behind him. Despite the invitation he remained standing.

Mary looked at him, then kneeling in front of him and taking his hand in hers.

"John, you must trust me, I will, I promise this as your friend. I will tell you everything upon arrival in France. I fear speaking here, Janet is a good girl, but we have no choice, we will have to leave her here, in charge of the apartment."

"But madame, if we are being watched, if we are seen leaving, we will be followed, by whom? By how many? Think on this, does Bothwell have Huguenot allies in France?" He stared at the ceiling in despair. "Oh, these religious wars!" then returning to the matter at hand, "Madame, how can we leave un-noticed?" John felt embarrassed, he had overstepped his position and was about to ask for forgiveness.

Mary stood then returned to her clothes. Then after a short while of awkward silence. Set down the clothes, she sat on the bed thinking, she turned to look at John and smiled.

"John, do you remember happier times, when I and our Queen, would mix with the common folk of the mile?"

John looked at her in confusion,

"Well yes, of course I do madame, as you and our queen stand as tall as any man. You both would dress as men of the city, and.." he paused then spoke slowly as he realised. "Pass through the crowded mile unnoticed, the people of the town, unaware, that her Majesty and her Lady in Waiting were amongst them." Mary stood up and from her wardrobe pulled out a suit of male clothing, a dark knee length tunic with gold piping on the shoulders and matching gold buttons, after she laid the coat on the bed, she drew out a pair of black leggings, folding them over her arm, she turned and smiled at John.

"If our queen and I could pass as men of the town, then we can pass as two gentlemen of France hurrying to the harbour to catch our voyage as we simply wish to return home, we can board the ship unnoticed. I shall do the talking as you have no French" John nodded in submission.

After the luggage had been collected, The two men of France, walked down the Mile, the trunk had been sent ahead with two willing couriers, very willing, after John had promised a large tip. The sun was high and full in the midday sky. John gestured to Mary, his hand open as he walked along- side her urging her to advance, ahead of him. She shook her head. The silent conversation confirming to John that they were simply two gentlemen, and not, mistress and servant. John watched her in her dark tunic and leggings, plain sturdy black shoes, her cloak billowing slightly due to her long strides, in spite the calmness of the day.

As he walked, Johns' attention was drawn to a plain brown carriage being pulled by two horses. It seemed to slow as it passed them, was it following them, there was no crest or name on the side. John cursed himself and held his dagger hilt.

"Madame" he whispered, without turning his head or stare.

Mary responded in an equal whisper, John listening closely to hear, staring directly ahead she replied.

"I am aware of it, continue John, it has been there since we left home."

"Yes madame," As the carriage continued past, Mary stopped and turned to John, speaking sharply, almost scolding him.

"You must stop calling me Madame?

"Yes mada…" John felt stupid, if he could not understand this instruction, what help was he going to be, "What shall I call you then?"

Mary thought for a second,

"My dear father was named James, let us use the French version Jacques, as we are French?"

"Certainly, (pauses) Jacques."

Mary walked away from him down the hill that is the mile, John was unsure, Jacques? addressing her by a single name, walking by her side, not behind at a respectful distance. It just didn't feel correct to him.

Once they were in the harbour, a brown carriage with no labelling stood by the harbour office, John stopped, was it the same carriage from before? He just wasn't sure. Mary spoke under her breath.

"There are many carriages in the city John. Quickly, show me our ship, then attend to the luggage."

Approaching their ship, La Dauphine, Mary greeted the captain in flawless French, John remained silent, merely bowing towards the captain when his name was mentioned. After what, to John seemed an age, Mary began to board, John despite feeling relieved to be on board. He continued to look all around as they were led to their cabin. Ever aware of the danger they were now both.

Later that evening, after the boat had set sail and was heading towards the open waters of the English-channel. Mary and John remained nervous. They sat, silently, in their cabin. The noise of the sea, cries of the crew, the creaking of the boat adding to the sound of the flapping sails.

Mary had changed into a dress, John remained in his sombre attire. The silence was broken abruptly by knocking on the cabin door.

The two travellers looked at each other, then John, indicating to Mary for silence approached the cabin door.

"Who calls? Can a man not have privacy on his voyage, what is the meaning of this disturbance?"

John set his ear against the door, awaiting a reply.

"John, it is I, Charles Martell, can an old friend not visit you John, come now open the door."

John took a step back from the door as Mary rose from her chair and retreated as far as possible in the cabin. John sniffed the air, a strange, yet familiar scent, filling his nostrils.

"Forgive me sir," he called out as his fingers danced on the hilt of his dagger, "I failed to recognise your voice. I was unaware of your presence on this craft" He looked over at Mary, who shook her head as his hand went to the door key causing him to pause.

"Dumfries, my friend, as you know I am friends with your servant Janet, such a nice young girl, it would be a tragedy if anything were to happen to her, with you, and your mistress, being away from home." John stared at Mary, then without thinking, quickly unlocked the door and pulled it open. Standing before him was Charles Martell, the blonde man with the cold eyes from earlier in the ticket office. John was unsure of what to do for a second, then he decided.

Without speaking a warning, John punched Martell hard in his throat, causing him to fall backward, then John advanced on him. Pulling closed the door behind him.

Mary rose from her hiding place, she approached the door and placing her ear against it. She could hear the sound of a scuffle happening outside it. She looked around the cabin for a weapon. But saw none. Then she was startled, a loud splashing noise could be heard. Then silence, she swallowed air, her hand hovered by the door lock. Then Johns voice, barely above a whisper.

"Madame, please it is I, unlock the door, we are safe, for now." Mary opened the door; Johns' face was bloodied and his collar torn. He raised his hand to indicate he was fine.

"What happened?" she asked as he entered the cabin.

"Our problem is dealt with." We all have our secrets ma'am, Mary was unsure, John looked injured, concerned, she raised her hand to the developing bruising on his face. He turned from her.

"I am fine madame. Please." Mary lowered her hand and withdrew from him. She had held a secret from him, the reason for the journey. He was entitled to his. John had disposed of their problem, maybe she should just be grateful to him for that.

For the remaining voyage, the weather remained fair. Mary had remained, for the most part of the journey, in the cabin, away from prying eyes. John remained outside, almost a sentry.

"Madame?" John began one morning over breakfast.

"Jacques" she replied with a smile.

His mouth came close to a smile.

"My point madame James. If we are pass safely to our destination. It is not possible that Bothwell spies will be looking for a lady and her servant. We may be ahead, may not be? If there was one on the boat, others could be ahead, waiting for us?" Considering this for a moment. Mary replied.

"I shall change."

Martell struggled in the sea; the cold had shocked him as it ripped him to his core. His clothes felt heavy, and he was not a strong swimmer. He could only watch as the Dauphine sailed away into the darkness, leaving him stranded. Where were the ships crew, surely one of them would have heard the splash. He truly felt this was his time, to drown in the open sea, cold, wet and alone. Then he heard voices behind him, he turned, desperately trying to keep his head above water, a ship, small, but a ship.

"Hey, hey! Over here, please."

A light at the side, two people pointing towards him, shouting back over their shoulder. Then a third person, he swam for the craft, as he did, he heard a small splashing sound, a rope! Thrown from the boat. He was saved. Who these people were, he did not care, soon he was pulled on board and found himself hunched over, shivering? Staring up at three confused faces.

As the journey progressed, the days, and nights, continued peacefully. Despite this, John remained a sentry outside the cabin, standing guard, refusing access to anyone who came near, whether an enemy or simply a curious sailor, intrigued by the unseen passenger holed up inside the cabin. All approaches were rejected, politely and firmly. In two languages.

As the days bled into weeks the ship made slow going as calm conditions, though welcome by all caused a long voyage to stretch. Mary yearned for the sunlight and calm sea breeze but, John advised her to remain hidden. She knew he was right, the letter she now had tucked into her under dress was too valuable and dangerous to fall into the wrong hands. In her cabin she waited as the long hours wore her spirit down.

After over two weeks of sailing, she knew the French coast was nearby. Mary was desperate to stand on deck and watch as it came into view. She also knew it was impossible. From her cabin she could feel the movement in the boat, peering out of the small porthole. She sighted a storm coming from behind them, catching the boat, coming close.

As night fell, she could feel and hear the storm engulf the craft, the wind causing the sails to billow and stretch, the noise of the sailors yelling to each other on deck caused her nerves to fail her. What if they sank, before retiring to bed she thought of the letter, she knelt and prayed for safe passage for the ship, its crew, John and herself.

"John!" she found herself breaking the silence of the cabin. Where was he, was he safe. She rose and leapt towards the door. Caring little of herself or who may have been watching outside. There he was. Huddled on the deck against the cabin door frame. Soaking wet, shivering, dagger still in hand.

"John, come inside, you will die out here!" she found herself yelling as the noise of the storm began to rise. He looked up at her,

"Madame I'm fine, get yourself inside before someone sees."

Mary almost laughed, was he noble or stubborn?

"Who is paying any attention to us as we enter this storm?"

"Madame please!" he implored her "Return inside the cabin!"

"Not without you!" she replied as she grabbed his cloak and tried to haul him inside. As she did this a wave crashed against the boat, sending Mary backward into the cabin and off her feet. John jumped at once and ran to help.

Once he had aided her to her feet, Mary seized the moment and rushed to close the door.

"Now Dumfries, I am ordering you as your Mistress, to remain inside this cabin, also remove those sodden clothes before you catch your death!"

John blushed at the thought of undressing here, but her use of his surname made him realise that she would not change her mind on this.

"Madame as you instruct, I shall obey but, undress, here." he gestured around the cabin, "in front of you, it would not be appropriate."

"John!" Mary snapped back, "I will turn my back and close my eyes, there is some of your male attire in the chest, remove those wet clothes and change this instant," she paused, "Please."

John agreed to do her bidding, he roughly pulled off his cloak, then, slowly and nervously whilst glancing at Mary's turned back removed his sodden shirt, britches and tights.

He raised the lid of the chest then stepped behind it. Using it as a shield for his embarrassment. Looking away from Mary and into the chest he saw only feminine attire, he felt unsure even touching it as he moved Mary's clothing to one side, but the cold he now felt spurred him on. Finally, he found a male night shirt, which he pulled over himself as quickly as he could.

"Madame," he whispered, "I am as decent as I am going to be." Mary turned and looked at him, suppressing a smile, she pointed towards the bed,

"Into bed John before you catch cold, you are no use to me sick."

"Madame, I must protest, this is your cabin and that," pointing at the bed, "is your bed, I simply could not possibly," he stammered, unsure of what to say next. "What would people think or say?"

Mary grinned towards the floor, "John, the only people here are you and I, it shall be our little secret. Now you take that side I shall have this." She said pointing to the side nearest her.

John was agog, "Madame! You intend to sleep in the bed!" struggling to comprehend the situation, "With me!" lowering his voice "Madame it is not right."

Loosing patient, Mary almost barked. "John Dumfries, what is or is not right does not matter right now, I have no intention of sleeping on the floor, and I refuse to let you. Now get into bed and sleep." She smiled to him, "Do not worry, I don't snore."

John looked confused, "Madame, how do you know? You have never been married."

Mary laughed out loud, "No John, but I have been betrothed," she smiled to herself, then under her breath, "a few times."

Reluctantly John slid into the bed but slept little.

Throughout the night the sea caused the boat to sway from one side to the other, adding to Johns nerves, lying in a bed with his mistress, they were not married or even betrothed, this was simply not correct. The wind and rain rose in strength, causing to John to feel sick. He looked over at Mary, eyes closed in a peaceful sleep. How was this possible? He threw his legs out of the bed, went to stand but as he did so, the whole boat lurched to one side, he was thrown against the cabin wall, then turned to balance, falling forward, he found himself sprawled across the bed, his face lying on Marys' chest, waking her.

Mary sat up, looked at Johns panic-stricken face and tried not to laugh.

"John, back to your side of the bed I think," John jumped up, and reeled backwards,

"Madame I am so, so sorry, the boat it moved, it caught me off guard, I must apologise madame, I meant no, no." He did not know what he meant, he found himself standing before her, half naked and fully embarrassed.

Mary laughed softly, yet despite being tempted to prolong his torture she controlled herself.

"John, please turn your back, an accident is an accident, I shall rise and dress, with this storm around us, neither will sleep tonight." John bowed his head and turned away from her.

Mary stood, dressing in her male clothing, turned to John.

When both were dressed, Mary looked on in disbelief as John insisted on wearing his, still damp, clothing, the pair ventured outside and soon wished they had not. The storm had increased, their vision was blinded by the water of the waves pounding the craft.

They had barely made a few feet when a huge wave hit them both, sending them onto their knees, drenched and gasping for air, above the din John yelled at Mary.

"Madame, we must get inside, for our safety." Mary looked up at him as he rose and steadied himself, he reached out a hand towards her, which she gratefully accepted.

Once returned to the cabin, a panic engulfed Mary, the letter, where was it? She searched her clothing frantically, it had been inside her tunic, she was certain, she liked to keep it close to her heart, she had since her Queen had given her it. John looked at her smiling.

"Madame, yours?" Mary knew he was taking revenge for her earlier teasing, but she was so relieved to see the letter in his hand, still dry, she immediately forgave him.

"Thank you, John," they stood in silence, then both jumped as a knocking arrived at the door.

John indicated for Mary to move away from the entrance as he approached it.

"Who calls upon us?" A voice responded.

"C'est moi le Captaine, j'ai besoin de te parler" a French voice called through the wooden door. Mary stepped forward.

"It is the captain, he needs to talk with us, please open the door." John touched his dagger, to reassure himself it was there, then opened the cabin door, inviting in a tall, thin man, his skin toughened from years at sea, his eyes still bright, a rough beard covering his face. His clothing workman like, his rough shirt and leggings were brown as was his full-length cloak, all were soaked through. He shivered as he entered, dipping his head slightly to John then to Mary, sea water dripping from his hat onto the floor.

He continued to talk in French to Mary, John understanding little stood back a pace watching. As he turned to leave, he looked at John and speaking in English,

"Your colleague will inform you of the news, good day sir."

John looked at Mary who sat on the bed, a worrying look on her face.

"John," she took a deep breath, "The captain has informed me that the storm has blown us off course," John stepped forward about to speak, Mary raised a hand to stop him.

"We will still land in France, but not in Roscoff, the captain is going to land in Francipolis, Le Harve. It is nearer but not where we had planned." John considered this.

"Well madame, If we are to land sooner we can depart this damn boat and rid ourselves of these terrible seas, also," he grinned at the thought.

Mary thought on this, "Plus, if Bothwell spies think we are to land in Roscoff, then he will have no-one in Le Harve awaiting us, perhaps, we can gain time on him as we make haste to Rouen."

"Rouen?" questioned John, "is this to be our final destination?"

Mary sighed, then "yes John it is our destination, Once there, I must find and demand an audience with the Duke, I have a letter from the Queen herself, which I must ask, beg him to take to the French king himself. It is of utmost importance for our queen, John I beg your silence and help."

John nodded silently, then after considering, "we had best prepare Madame, for our journey to Rouen.

"That is true John, true, let us pack our things, the captain intends to land in Le Harve soon, we must be ready.

The final days, for John, were agony, the weather had improved, and the sea was calm, but with the coast, and dry land, in sight, the hours seemed to turn into days, days into weeks.

Then, finally, in sight, the harbour, Le Harve, not Roscoff, as originally planned, but for John, his nightmare was over. Once docked, he and Mary, both dressed as respectable gentlemen in tights, britches and tunics, dark waist length cloaks pushed over their shoulders in respect of the warm evening. John descended first, once on the jetty, he felt a desire to kneel down and kiss it. He looked down. Under his brown leather boots was a rough wooden jetty, filthy with dirt and scraps of raw fish, it was a desire he could easily resist. Mary followed him, she smelt the air, a mix of sea, fish and a faint smell of a town, up ahead she could see a cross, the chapel Notre Dame, part church part construction site as the work had begun to replace the old wooden structure, a church so drab, thought Mary, it could only be improved by turning away from it, with a stone replacement, a bell tower was stretching itself, stone by stone into the evening sky. No-one was in sight at the church, Mary wanted to take Mass and confession, but what would John say? She looked at him.

"Madame?" He said the word, as a question, Mary looked up into his eyes. Smiling,

"John, we have arrived safely, can you find accommodation, an inn for the night."

"Madame," John looked concerned. "Can I suggest, we make haste, find horses or a carriage, travel to Rouen as soon as is possible, surely?" Mary raised her hand gently to silence him. Placing it upon his chest.

"John, no-one is in more of a rush then I, but to travel, just two of us, through the dark night on roads, of which we are unsure. It would be foolish if not downright dangerous. We have to stay here for tonight. Then, at first light we travel. Do you understand?" John nodded and sighed to himself; he knew she was right.

"Yes madame, I shall head into the town to secure," He paused and smiled. "Two chambers for the night." Mary smiled.

Le Harve

"Thank you, John, I shall join you later, there is something I must do first." John understood what she meant, she walked away from him, leaving him on the jetty, then realising he had a job to do he walked towards what he presumed was the town.

Unknown to John, was that, a pair of cold blue eyes widened in surprise as they sighted Mary and John depart the Dauphine. The eyes belonging to Charles Martell, the man John thought he had disposed of mid channel. Martell hid himself behind a barrel. Watching, unable to believe his luck, he had only stopped off in Le Harve to rest his horse, and himself after the small vessel of his rescue had taken him to Calais. He had stolen a horse and had Intended to continue traveling the coast road to Roscoff in the morning, where the ship was due to dock. But this? "How fortunate, someone in heaven must like me". He smirked "But not for long." He smiled to himself, watching as Mary headed in one direction, her servant the other. She was alone, unprotected. He rubbed his throat. Then decided this was too good an opportunity to miss. He then decided and guessing where Mary was headed. He returned to his accommodation, to collect something he was about to need.

Mary knelt in the unfinished cathedral, in front of the golden, unfinished alter-piece, Queen Marys' rosary beads in one hand, her eyes closed, as she knelt in prayer.

She felt a presence, but not a religious one, movement. She was definitely not alone. She saw the reflection in the gold of the alter, from her puffed sleeve she withdrew a small knife, throwing herself to the side, she threw, she missed.

"Rather unladylike Mary," Martell stood in front of her, loaded crossbow directly towards her, she gulped as she stared into those cold eyes, his intention clear. Then in an instance Martell was floored. John, he must have followed. He flattened Martell onto the stone floor, then pulled his dagger.

"John No! not here never in a church of God." She raised herself and ran over to her confused servant, grabbing the weapon out of his hand.

"No John! Never in a house of God."

Mary ran from the Cathedral leaving John standing over Martell, confused, but he knew his duty and where his loyalty lay, he grabbed the crossbow from Martell. Then followed Mary out, running to catch up.

Mary stopped, she needed Johns' protection more than ever now for if the bowman had an accomplice. Also, she was desperate to be in the safety of their lodgings, but as she had gone straight to the Cathedral, she did not know where they were.

The two returned to the lodgings John had secured, As Mary slept, John sat at the end of her bed, crossbow in one hand, their travel chest pushed up against the door. His other fist gripping his dagger staring at the door handle. Ready to respond if anyone tried to enter.

At first light, he gently shook Marys' foot, waking her.

"We had better prepare to leave Madame, it is light outside."

"Thank you, John," she said with a tired voice, "Prepare the horses, it's time to journey to Rouen.

Mary rose with the sun and dressed in male travelling clothes and waited for John to fetch the horses.

Then, after paying the inn keeper, she stood outside enjoying the morning sunshine, her eyes looking around the street all the time, fear of the assassin still praying on her mind.

She turned and saw the transport John had arranged. A horse and cart.

"Is this it? I thought you getting horses John? A pair" She blurted out.

"John, sitting upon the front of the cart, looked amazed.

"I did madam, what do you think this is?" he responded.

"A horse John, one, I thought we were getting two?"

John breathed deeply, "Madame, where would the luggage go?"

Mary blushed then giggled. "That is a fair point."

They began their journey in silence.

The day passed as slowly as the road, as Johns' horse was nor the fastest, but it did it's best. Ploughing on regardless of hills and streams and rough roads.

Until, a problem, the company had been following the river towards their destination but after a few hours they soon realised they needed to cross it. On their side of the river the road simply stopped, it continued on the other side. No bridge, no crossing, no ferry, without this they were stuck. Darkness began to creep around them.

John halted the cart, then jumping down looked as far as possible in both directions.

Looking at Mary, "Madame, we never passed a crossing, did we?"

"No John, I'm sure one of us would have noticed."

John turned his gaze quickly back up the road,

"John, are you all right? What is it?"

He walked slowly passed the cart in the direction from whence they came,

"Wait here Madame please, I think we are being followed."

He walked off into the surrounding darkness, Mary turned and watched him go. Unsure and afraid. She could hear voices, she searched herself for her knife, then remembering the Church, began to search the cart.

Nothing.

Out of the darkness John returned, hands behind his head, his mouth trying to convey a message to Mary in silence. A message she could not understand, she lifted the reins for the horse, unsure whether she should flee. Leaving John. Could she? No, never, they had left Edinburgh mistress and servant, but they were a team now, maybe even friends. Then she saw him. Martell.

He walked behind John the tip of Marys' dagger pressed into Johns back.

"My lady Seton, we meet again,"

He grinned as he pushed John against the cart.

"Despite the attire, I would recognise you anywhere, you are really making an easy job terribly hard."

Mary laughed,

"I am so sorry if saving my own life is inconveniencing you sir."

"Madame, please now is not the time for your humour." John pleaded.

Martell pressed the blade against Johns' throat.

"Very true sir, perhaps if you Papists taught your women their place we wouldn't be in this far off place, far from home."

John considered his next move,

"Sir, I am no papist." Then a strange voice, with a heavy accent spoke out.

"If he is no Papist, then he is a brother of mine." Martell dropped the weapon as four armed horsemen surrounding the cart, dressed in sombre black, britches, tights, boots and cloaks. Mary knew exactly who they were, Huguenots.

Under the circumstances, they were, for her, an unusually welcome sight. Mary spoke using French, "Sir we are two humble men, travellers, just trying to make our way to Rouen when this stranger availed us. I believe he is a robber sir, can you help a fellow," with this she had to pause, in her pocket her hand touched her royal rosaries. "convert, to the new faith."

John looked on as did Martell, both had little French but John knew his mistress was talking them into safety. The man who looked to their leader, considered this, then pointed to Martell.

"You sir," he said in English to Martell, "Speak French?" Martell shook his head.

The Huguenot leader leaned forward in his saddle, then gave his company orders in French.

Martell looked at John with a pleading look.

"John please, you know I am no Papist, help me." John turned his back as two of the horsemen dismounted, gathered rope and tied Martell, despite his protests, struggles and pleads, to the nearest tree.

The leader moved his horse closer to the cart and Mary.

"We are Huguenots, as I am sure you know, the war is" he paused, "at peace, albeit an armed peace, these roads are no place for travellers alone, we will escort you, our brothers to safety, but we may not enter Rouen, it is a papist place, you would both be wise not to enter."

"I have important business there sir, too important to ignore." Mary responded, "I must take my chances."

The leader laughed,

"As long as you do not take mass sir." The others laughed, even John managed a smile, Mary laughed nervously as the four took up position, in pairs ahead of and behind the cart and with their armed guard at the ready they headed to Rouen.

The sun began to rise, as did the mood of Mary and John, for in the distance they saw the spire of a cathedral, despite it being many years since Mary had laid eyes on it, she knew the cathedral was Notre Dame de Rouen, they were so close now, but then their guards stopped.

"We go no further than here." The Leader said to the pair as they drew their cart to a halt.

"Why?" Mary asked, then after a pause, "If I may ask why sir, please we are so close."

"This," it was his turn to pause, "this town is held by the Papists Madame, if we were to enter, it would be the death of us, and possibly both of you." He replied pointing at Mary and John.

Mary rose upward on the cart seat, "Good sir, I am truly grateful for your assistance, but I must continue."

"What business is so important, you are willing to risk death for it?" the leader interrupted.

"My business sir, sorry, please accept my apologies but it is my business." An awkward pause fell upon them, the leader looked at his men then at Mary. To break the silence John spoke.

"My good friend, perhaps as a token of our gratitude, you would accept some form of payment, we have money."

The leader turned to John as he searched in his clothing for his purse.

"Money!" he said almost shouting, "we have no wish for any of your money. My friend, a chance to help is all we wish or deserve, God speed and keep the true faith my friends, let us hope we meet again when we will have prevailed, but mark my words." He spoke directly to Mary, "That cathedral is a den of corruption and faithlessness, watch your backs. For one slip, there will be a knife in it."

He turned his horse away from the cart and shouting an order in French to his men, led them away, back up the road. Mary and John watched as they faded out into the distance. Both looked out into the empty road allowing the still quiet to consume them.

"John I am beginning to feel the cold, let us proceed."

"Into that town Madame?" John asked, Mary could hear the tremble in his voice.

"Yes John, that town."

John slowed the horse as they approached the towns, Gatehouse. Two sentries approached, backed up by two more on top of the tower, crossbows at the ready. Mary called out to them in joyful French, one of the guards, nodding slightly, replied in French, the other guard walked around the cart, patting the horse as he did so. He stopped next to John, eyed him, or rather his sombre puritan attire, then called out to his comrade. The two came together, in front of the horse. Talking in voices so low, that Mary had to lean forward as she tried to listen.

"Madame?"

"John shush, I cannot hear."

"Madame please, are we safe?"

The guard approached John,

"Votre lame monsieur" he said, his hand out-stretched.

John looked at him blankly, the guard spoke again, impatience in his voice.

"Votre lame monsieur!"

John turned to Mary, she responded quickly.

"John, your blade, your dagger, give it to him, all those who enter the city must disarm.

"Are you sure, we should, there will be danger here and we are strangers, and let us not forget our friend from Le Harve."

"John," she said placing a hand on his arm, our mission here is too important, please hand him your dagger.

"Are you sure Madame?"

Mary turned and looking him in the eye, "Yes I am."

Reluctantly and slowly, John withdrew his blade and handed it, handle first to the guard.

"Entrer," yelled the guard, as Mary rubbed her rosary for luck the portcullis rose slowly in front of them, screaking and yelling its effort as it did so.

Finally, to Marys relief, and Johns trepidation, they entered the town. Rouen, they had arrived. The first part over, as John urged the horse forward, he turned to Mary.

"Madame, what now?" Mary laughed. Patting John on the arm,

"I don't know John; I simply do not know."

Martell was still struggling and crying out for help, when a sound silenced him, "A horse," he thought, "help"

He yelled out in English, damninng himself as he did not know the word in French.

A horseman stopped on the path next to the trees.

"You sir," He called out in English, "Are you being held captive?"

"Sir," Martell replied, "My friend, robbers, bandits, they have taken my horse and my money, they have left me here to die. Please I need help, I implore you."

The stranger considered this, then dismounted, walking his horse towards Martell.

As he drew a knife, Martells eyes opened wide, was he about to finish him, Surely no.

He didn't, he cut Martells binds with his knife. Then stuck it into the tree as Martell grabbed him in thanks.

"You sir, are free now, Rouen is but a short trip away, there are people there who will assist you, I hop you find your robbers and your property." The stranger turned, as he did, Martell grabbed the knife and plunged it into his back.

The stranger fell, Martell wiped the blade clean, then gently soothed the horse as the strange man approached it.

Climbing on, he took the reins and led the horse away.

"Bandits and robbers," Martell joked to himself, "They're everywhere," laughing he spurred the horse forward.

Rouen

A few days passed and they were both feeling annoyed and unsure by their situation, accommodation had been secured next to the town cathedral. Their lodgings for the foreseeable future, a small apartment. Up from the street by means of a small tight stone stair which led to a heavy green door, rounded at the top, causing both to have to dip their heads upon entry. A small greeting chamber giving a view of the cathedral vegetable garden. Old uncomfortable wooden furniture. Blackened fireplace. A scullery and two smelly bedrooms. Low ceilings. Outdoor privy, but cheap and private. Also, much to Marys' delight and to Johns' mistrust the cathedral was so close. He would sit after dinner, on the small rough stool by the window and watch as the huge gothic monument to, as he saw it, the old religion, would disappear into the darkening night. He felt alone in a strange country and town, he was picking up a few words of the language faster then he had thought he would, but whenever they ventured out of their home, Mary would take over any conversation. He knew his place. But, despite this, after a lot of persuasion, Mary had finally told him of the reason behind their journey and the importance of the letter.

Mary also felt unsure of their situation. The small lodgings were basic to Mary, she had lived a life of palaces, hunting lodges, servants, and grand estates as a lady in waiting to royalty. To find herself in this simple abode was alien to her. But it was a warm, secure sanctuary for them both. Attempts to see the duke had to be abandoned. For they had learned the terrible news. the Duke, upon whom so much relied, was dead, killed in a hunting accident.

"What now?" was all John could think, he knew of the letter, but with no-one to hand it to, surely, they would be returning home. He rose from his chair and began, much to Marys' annoyance pacing the room.

"Impossible" Said Mary, "Bothwell will know we travelled here, if we return to Edinburgh, he will have us both arrested, and do," she paused, "I dare not to think what he is prepared to do, to find out the reason for our journey. I'm sorry John, but we are both in danger over this, besides I simply could never face her Majesty, our Queen if I have failed."

"But Madame, the Duke is dead, it is not a failure by you or I, we are victims of a circumstance not of our making."

Mary thought on this, "What of the Duchess?"

John stopped his pacing, "The who?"

Mary stood, looking at John, "The duke was married, the Duchess is still alive, will she not be in control of the Dukedom until any children they have are of age? I believe, if we can gain an audience with her, we have a chance, yes, I know a small chance but, John." She was almost pleading with him, "Please I need your help and protection, let me try this one last time, if we fail, I swear we will return home, you have my word."

John nodded in agreement, for him her word was always good enough. "Tomorrow, we find your Duchess." Saying this as he left the room.

Mary sat down, placing her head into her hands, "Than you John," then to herself, "My friend"

The Constable

Mary walked slowly towards the Ducal palace, her stomach was full of nerves, so full she refused all breakfast. Now, she walked through the courtyard of the palace, a meeting with the Duchess was not arranged. But after the passing of their remaining coins to guards and Ducal servants, she had managed to arrange a meeting with a man called Padgett, also known as The Constable, most senior man in the Dukedom, after the Ducal family. His reputation for stubbornness was well known and as Mary had learned form the townsfolk, he had a deep mistrust, near hatred of women. This was going to be a difficult morning.

The Ducal Palace was a true palace, grand wide staircases led to opulent chambers on several floors. Servants ran around in exquisite red and gold coats complete with black britches, starkly clean white stockings, polished shoes clicking on the marble floors as they hurried to their tasks, art adorned the walls, Dukes of centuries past looked down upon you, faces almost saying "Know your place."

Mary was led into a grand room, ceiling high windows bathing the room in sunlight. Thick, elegant red coloured drapes pulled back by golden ropes either side of them, bar one, which hung loose. There behind a gold writing table sat Padgett, the man known as the Constable. As Mary was formally introduced by the page at her side. He barely noticed. Made no attempt at a greeting, remaining seated reading the document in his hands. Mary curtsied politely, falling onto one knee awaiting him, her hand held aloft for him to accept as greeting. Looking up and embarrassed. She rose and coughed politely. He finished reading before he acknowledged her.

He stood now, a short rather fat man, a reddened face with plain features, small eyes around a large nose and thin mouth. He stood out in the palace. He was the first ugly thing Mary had seen since she arrived.

"Madame Seton, I believe" he almost shouted across the room towards her. Mary again curtsied and raised her hand for him take but he simply sat again, gesturing Mary to do likewise in the empty chair. As Mary sat, he picked up another document and started to read again.

Mary decided to take control from his rudeness,

"Constable," she said, smiling politely if "I could have your attention for a short time. I have a request and am told you are the," she paused, "Gentleman, to discuss it with."

The Constable looked up from his paper, he had heard her pause before "Gentleman." And understanding her sarcasm eyed Mary coldly,

"A short time is all I have, so quickly please."

Mary breathed, "My good sir I have travelled from Edinburgh with a letter for the Duke."

The Constable interrupted her at once, "My good" it was his turn to pause, "Lady. The Duke is dead, it would appear you have had a wasted trip."

"But sir, please, the duchess is alive and well, is she not. I wish an audience with her."

This time the Constable stood and leaned over his desk,

"Madame, the Duchess is in mourning for her husband, she is not to be bothered by a mere messenger!"

"My good man," Mary spat back rather too loudly, "I am Lady Seton daughter of Lord Seton the sixth and Marie Pierres. Also, I am the Granddaughter of Rene Pierres of Plessis Baudouin, and my letter is from none other than Her Highness Mary, the Queen of Scots!"

"Oh my!" he said in sarcasm, "Why didn't you say so, the Queen no less?"

Mary stood from her chair her temper lit. "Yes Sir, I am Mary Seton, Lady in Waiting to the queen Herself!"

The Constable sat back down laughing to himself, "I do not know who you truly are madame, but do you expect me to believe that a Queen would send a mere woman as her messenger? Be away with you, you're short time has now ended." With that he rang a small bell and a guard entered the room.

Mary stood, telling herself, "Do not bow!" She turned from him then as she walked from the room, grinned to herself.

"Constable?"

"Yes" he replied without looking up,

"Please help, for as I am a mere woman, and not capable to carry out the difficult task of delivering a letter, would you allow a man to deliver my letter.

The constable leaned back in his chair, thinking, Mary kept her back to him.

"It would be considered more appropriate, why?"

Turning to face him, "My brother arrives in the morning, perhaps he would be permitted an audience? If that was more to your liking."

"Your brother, tomorrow, that is convenient."

Mary flashed a smile, towards his face of stone, "It is rather, isn't it. I will send him to you after breakfast, good day sir." She left the room as quickly as not appearing to run dictated.

Once out of the room, the constable spoke over his shoulder,

"Now sir, I have abided by your request," He held out his hand as a bag of coins was set gently into it, he then turned and looked up at Martell, who had been hiding in the room the whole time.

"I will have a message sent to my Lord Bothwell advising him of your assistance." He replied bowing to the constable,

"I hope there be no unfortunate incidents between you Scots in my town." Martell standing upright,

"It will be discreet sir. I assure you."

Returning to their lodgings she found John waiting, with tea and impatience.

"Madame, you must tell me all, I am worried for you, our letter and myself. Please I implore you, are you to meet the Duchess?"

"No John," then seeing Johns anguished face, "Fear not, for my brother will."

His face turned to confusion, "Brother madame, what brother?"

Mary smiled, then walked over to the chest, opened it leant into it then found what she required, she turned to face John holding aloft the britches she wore in Edinburgh,

"This brother." It was Johns turn to smile.

The Duchess

The next morning, bright and early, two gentlemen of Edinburgh walked side by side, underneath a sunrise almost as picturesque as the city of Rouen.

"Mad.....James, do we know what awaits us? What we are to say, I am unarmed, what if?"

Mary stopped and looked directly at John.

"My friend, I simply do not know, but we have courage and ingenuity on our side. When it is needed an idea will propose itself." Smiling she continued towards the palace. John stood for a moment, considering for a moment, how little he knew, how little control he had.

Outside the Constables chamber they waited, and waited, then waited some more, their stomachs both growling a reminder it was nearing lunch. About to give up the Constable appeared before them.

"Scottish men I believe?", he grinned a smug self smile.

Before a visibly annoyed Mary could reply John interrupted,

"My Lord, that is correct, we are, as you correctly say, the Scottish men, here on a mission from our Queen. We plead with you sir and request a meeting with the Duchess." He paused then almost blurting out, "If she is available of course." John bowed then presented his hand to the Constable to shake, he looked at it but did not shake it. Mary spoke up.

"Sir, I am," she paused, "James, 7th Earl of Seton, I believe you have met my sister, the good lady Mary."

The Constable smirked, "Yes briefly, rude, obnoxious, woman, perhaps your family did not teach her, her true place as a woman." He turned his back to the pair as Mary looked around for something she could hit him with, then suddenly to their surprise.

Clicking his fingers he turned to the pair,

"Well now please, we must not keep the Duchess waiting."

John waited outside, feeling nervous as the constable insisted on leaving two guards to ensure John did indeed wait outside. Mary was led into an opulent and lavish anti chamber, then into a room resplendent with paintings, high ceilings, floor to ceiling windows, exquisite tapestries, wood flooring so polished she could see her reflection. But nothing of this beauty could prepare for the Duchess herself.

Into the room she walked, no glided, a tall woman of, maybe, thirty years, complete with an entourage of servants, the party stopped near Mary as she shed her cloak, glowing fire red hair cascaded from the underneath the hood onto bare milk white shoulders. Her dress of chalk white, decorated with wildflowers shrank at her small waist then widened onto the floor. She was a sight of pure beauty, Mary had never seen a human so perfect, not even her own Queen, she was stunned into silence. Her sharp green eyes surveyed Mary, then she smiled, a perfect smile, deep red lips parting to display perfect teeth which almost shone out at Mary, a porcelain hand rose to banish the servants, dismissing her entourage she turned and presented herself to Mary to greet.

Mary fell onto one knee and kissed it gently for fear it would break, she looked the Duchess, discreetly, form head to toe, the hair, the dress, bare shoulders, perfect heaving bosom, this was mourning? French style. She vowed a secret there and then, she liked it.

"Come sit sir," she indicated towards the seating, the giggled to herself. Mary stood, composing herself as the Duchess seemed to float toward and into her seat.

Mary sat on the edge of the chaise longue, the Duchess sat, barely causing a ripple on the cushions,

"Monsieur Seton," she turned away, covering her mouth to supress a giggle. "Monsieur, I believe you have a message for me?" Mary leaned back from her, unsure of herself but determined to complete her task for her queen.

"Yes madame, my, erm, sister and I have travelled from Scotland, Ecosse, on instruction of our queen, Mary, whom I believe, you and your late husband knew, we ask of you, no," Mary fell to her knees in front of the duchess, "We beg of you, assist us please, for our queen and your friend we beseech you madame, we have no one left to turn to."

The duchess smiled, gestured to her to retake her seat, then stared directly at Mary, making her nervous.

"My Lord Seton, I would like to say, it is so nice to have a man around to talk to, since my husbands passing, I miss the company of men. But please tell me," The Duchess leaned closer to Mary, "do all men of Scotland have such soft skin?" she reached up and with her fine fingers, stroked Marys cheek, "So soft, not a razer nick to be felt,

"Madame," Mary blushed, "I like to take care in my appearance, especially when meeting such esteemed company," Mary indicated to the Duchess, trying to regain her composure, the Duchess continued, "Your neck sir, is smooth and flat, no apple." Her hand stroked Marys throat, no apple there, Mary began to realise her ruse worked on some but not others.

The duchess began to smile a broad, mischievous grin. Her hand travelled into Mary's waistcoat and over her breasts.

"Madame," Mary was lost for words, her disguise seen through, yet the touch of this woman, she felt unsure of. She lifted the Duchess hand away from her, "Madame please. I have a message I must convey." The Duchess stood up and turning from Mary, spoke sharply and curtly.

"What is your name, woman! And what is it you want, Your disguise may fool men, such as the constable, but, men, men only see what they wish to see. But I see more, now be about your business or I shall call the guards." She stood by the window, the sunlight framing her.

Mary dropped her head, sighing she looked up, almost pleading, "Madame, please, I have a letter from Mary queen of Scots herself, she is in mortal danger with every passing day, she sent me here to beg your husband to petition the King for aid, but now I know the Duke is dead, I ask you, for pity for god for my Queen. If you refuse, I have failed and can never face my queen again," Mary began to wipe the tears she had no control of stopping, "I beg you madame, I am but a lowly servant of the queen, I care not for myself now, I may have already failed I am of no help. But you are a Duchess please help my queen." The Duchess pointed to a picture on the wall,

"My husband would have wanted to help you," she paused and smiled, looking away,

Then the Duchess looked directly at Mary, "so shall I, where is this letter?" Mary reached inside her sleeve and produced it. The duchess took it from her, Mary winced, as if in pain as she let it go, "This is for the King?" Mary nodded, The Duchess considered for a moment, tapping the letter of her hand. "If this is what you say, it is a letter from a Queen for a King, and I guarantee it shall remained unopened. I shall see to it that his highness receives it." Mary wanted to throw herself forward and kiss her feet.

"Madame how can I ever repay you?"

"You, My good lady Seton, shall do something for me, my husband, as you know is dead."

"Yes madame, a hunting accident" Mary was confused. Th Duchess continued,

"I do not believe it was an accident, I believe it was murder, by whom and why I do not know, but you, you Seton, you are new here, a fresh pair of eyes. I want you to prove it was murder and find my husband's killer or killers, do this for me and I will personally deliver this letter to our King." Silence befell the pair,

"Agreed?" Her left hand held the letter, her right extended for a handshake.

Mary stared in confusion, but soon realised, she had no other options.

Standing up, she shook her hand, "Yes madame, agreed."

Mary let go of her hand, then went to curtsy, realising, she straightened herself and performed a bow, of sorts. The duchess smiled, causing Mary embarrassment, she straightened, then walking backward, as she had always been taught to never turn her back on her social superior, headed for the door. Once through, she turned to the Constable and bowed with more aplomb. Then walked over to a waiting John.

"Well madame what happened?" he whispered,

"Outside please John," she said taking hold of his arm and shepherding him to the door.

Once outside of the palace and its prying eyes and ears,

"The Duchess and I have come to an agreement." After which she told John of the conversation

"You agreed to what?" Johns normal quiet determined manner had failed him as they walked from the Palace, "Madame are we not to return home? We are to investigate a murder that may not have been a murder, where do we start, who do we ask, why us?"

Mary stopped in the middle of the crowded street thinking.

"John I simply do not know."

Once outside Mary breathed in relief, things were progressing, not as she had planned, but, she was thinking that, in the Duchess, she had an ally. A powerful ally. She walked across the palace courtyard and out into the street, John following.

"Madame" he whispered; Mary gave no acknowledgement as she was so deep in her own thoughts.

"Madame!" he said it louder, then as he turned to ensure no-one was near, Mary tugged upon his arm.

"Come John" she spoke with authority but not scolding,

"We must get back to our lodgings and decide our next steps.

The pair walked in silence as they strode quickly alongside the long, thin cobbled alley that ran the full length of the vast cathedral. Then Mary stopped.

"Madame?" John whispered into her ear. She knew his question before he said it.

"John, do you see?" John, turned to one side and dipped his head to hide his face, looking from under the brim of his hat,

"Yes, I do."

There in front of them, barely a few steps, accompanied by two armed men stood Martell.

"This way John," Mary pulled him to one side and down the alley in the opposite direction from their temporary home. A brisk walk until,

Thay both heard the sound of following boots matching their pace, without consultation, the pair dived into the gathering crowds of Rouenaise then their brisk pace became a flight of flee.

They ran in unison across the street into the courtyard in front of Eglise St Maclou, too open thought Mary, as she looked for a place to hide, spotting one she grabbed John's hand,

"Quickly John, down here."

She dragged John between two buildings of Rouen, brick ground, topped for two or three floors with wooden structure, the main beams criss-crossing each other and painted black the spaces between laith and plaster, whitewashed in contrast.

They entered the small passage between them only to find their way blocked by another building, so closely were the buildings constructed.

"What now madame?" John spoke, barely audible.

"We cannot leave, Martell and his men are not far behind, we stay here, we stay quiet and we pray."

John went to speak but thought better of it, he simply nodded his understanding, the sound of running boots told of their pursuer's arrival. The running stopped, it became a slow pace, they were searching the area for them.

John and Marys eyes locked. So close to each other now, the brims of each other's hats overlapped.

John was unsure, he could feel Mary's chest breathing hard against his, she still held his hand, he could feel her breath on his lips, was he, no! He dispelled the thought from his mind, or tried to, was he aroused? No! She was his mistress his employer, she was also, of the old religion, he could, his god could, never allow it. He banished the idea from his head. Then turning his eyes out into the courtyard, silence.

He whispered to Mary.

"Gone?" He looked at her, she stared at him, her face a mystery.

"I'll go look." Mary nodded weakly, fearing for him and herself, she kept hold of his hand, John moved as slowly and as silently as he could, until the end of the alley, barely daring to breathe, he looked out, no-one in sight. He moved his other hand, placing it onto Marys and his own, an act of reassurance, for which of them he was unsure.

He reached for his dagger, of course it was not there. Feeling almost naked, hugging the side of the buildings, he led Mary out into the busy street, where using the crowds as cover, the pair walked slowly and silently towards their lodgings. Once there John locked and bolted the door, then ensured all the windows were likewise closed, before returning to the chamber where Mary sat on the old chair thinking.

"Well Madame" Mary looked up at him,

"Well, what?"

"This Investigation, where are we to begin?" Mary thought for a second, but as she rose to speak, there came a loud knock on the door.

Bravane

The two looked towards the front entrance, then at each other, had Martell found them?

"What now madame?" John whispered. "Who could that be?"

Mary looked at her servant with a look close to a glare,

"I do not know John, how about we open the door and find out" she replied sharply.

John held his tongue, then quickly went through to the scullery to find a knife, anything he felt he could use for defence. At last he found an old knife, old, missing its handle, but still sharp enough to do damage.

Mary stood by the door as the knock was repeated.

"Who calls please?" Mary holding the authority in her voice and the door key in her hand.

John gently moved her aside as he took up a position next to the door, as out of sight as the geography of the small hallway would allow.

"Madame Seton, I am Bravane, maid to the duchess, we met, briefly this morning. I have something for you, from the Duchess. Are you all-right madame?"

Mary sighed in relief, then, resting her head against the door and pushed the key into the lock. John reached over and touching her hand, shook his head as an instruction to wait.

"Are you alone Mademoiselle?" he called through the door.

"Why of course sir, my Duchess was most insistent I remain so."

John lifted his hand from Marys and nodded, pushing himself as far into the hallway corner as he could, with both hands, lifting his makeshift dagger high, ready to strike.

Mary unlocked and opened the door very slightly, peering out, the bright afternoon sunshine causing her to blink, it was the maid, and she was alone, but others could be hiding. She opened the door fully and pulled the servant inwards with sufficient force the unfortunate girl fell onto the stone floor where she saw John standing over her, blade in hand raised. She opened her mouth to scream but Mary, assessing the situation, fell to her knees in front of her,

"Young lady, mademoiselle, please do not be frightened, John will not harm you," she turned to John, still with blade raised, "He won't, will you John!"

John lowered his hand and the blade, with the other he offered to help the frightened young girl up.

"Forgive me young lady, how we may be of assistance? Please come through to our chamber."

Mary, still on the floor with her hand raised awaiting help, shook her head, raised herself and followed John and their guest.

The maid sat nervously looking between the two, who both stood over her.

"How can we be of assistance?" John repeated, the maid calmed herself,

"No sir, it is how I can be of assistance to you, my Lady, the Duchess sent me to give you this." From underneath her cloak she held forth a gift, Mary smiled, for it was a welcome gift, a large leather pouch, full, it would appear at first glance of livre, coins, money. Much welcome.

Mary controlled herself, and gently took the pouch, it was heavy, indeed livre, money.

Mary smiled,

"Young lady, please extend our deepest gratitude to your mistress, we will gratefully accept this" Mary paused, looking at John, "gift?"

"Yes Madame Seton, it is a gift from my lady, to assist you in your," she paused for the word, "investa?"

"Investigation," Mary finished for her.

"I must return to the palace now, I bid you adieu,"

Mary smiled, "And farewell to you to, our gratitude goes with you."

John saw her out then returned to the chamber to find Mary counting the coins.

"Well, that's one problem solved. Now all we have to do is find out if the Duke was murdered, why and by whom?" John stared at his mistress, his expression solemn, his head bowed.

"It would appear we are to stay here, in Rouen." He said, almost to the floor.

"Yes, my friend." John turned away from her to hide his disappointment, then Mary thought aloud.

"But to find out if and why, we first of all have to examine the Duke,

John was perplexed, turning he asked.

"Examine the Duke? But madame how? He is dead" realising, "No Madame no! it is ungodly!"

Mary looked at him, "We must find out where he is buried or entombed."

The Tomb.

They waited until nightfall, then walked through the darkened streets, with John holding aloft a lantern to light the way. After a short they arrived at St Ouen, a large gothic church, a mini cathedral, so close to it that when the sun shone, it lay in the great cathedrals shadow.

The two circled the church for a side entrance, finding one, John held the lantern out for Mary to hold as pulled out a crowbar, within seconds he had broken the lock and had pushed the door inward. He gestured for Mary to enter first, she did so, holding aloft the lantern, she moved it around the church, empty and silent. The lanterns light fell on pews, stone floor, then what she was looking for, the stairs, the stairs which led to the crypt, the Ducal crypt.

"John," she whispered, "Follow me please."

John followed as instructed, he was nervous, it was night, dark, and was entering illegally, entering a church of the old religion.

Mary hurried towards the stone stairwell, one hand, holding the lantern, the other taking the wooden railing.

Descending swiftly, John followed unsure of her plans, he sighed to himself, unsure of her plans, when was he ever sure of it?

Mary let the light guide her into the crypt, then she saw what she wanted, the Ducal family crypt, behind railings. In neat rows were stone coffins, she needed the newest, the current, no last Duke.

She approached the gate, locked.

"John, your assistance please," she whispered, pointing at the lock.

Hesitantly John used the crowbar to force open the lock, as he pulled gate open it emitted a loud squealing noise, the pair looked at each other, Mary touched his arm,

"Fear not John, we are alone here." John was not so sure,

"God is watching us, we are not alone." Mary smiled briefly, then pushed past into the crypt. She walked along the row of crypts until she found what she needed.

"John, this one" she said pointing to a crypt,

John breathed deeply,

"Madame please for the last time I implore you to think again."

"And for the last time John, I will not, we have no choice, please open it.

John placed the bar under the lip of the coffin lid, then pressing hard and closing his eyes in an attempt to push the thought of grave robbing from of his mind, heard the lid move.

He opened one eye, it was part opened, he pulled the bar out and pushed the lid as far over as he could, as it opened, he could smell the corpse, he was disgusted and felt sick. The stench as his own revulsion at himself, caused him to lurch, deep in his stomach.

Mary lowered the lantern closer to the body of the departed Duke.

"It's him John, I recognise him from the picture I saw at the Ducal palace. John look at this!"

John turned his back; the sight of the recently dead man was too much for him.

"Madame I would rather not, can we hurry, I wish to spend no longer here then I should."

"John, don't be so squeamish, quickly help open his tunic. I need to see the wound." Mary moved the Ducal flag, which wrapped the body, then began to unbutton his golden tunic. She began to run her hands over his chest and abdomen, John turned and appalled.

"Madame!" he almost shouted, "this is a corpse, this is tantamount to grave robbery."

"John," she said without stopping, "we are taking nothing but evidence, found it, here help me with the lantern as I open the shirt." Reluctantly he did so and held the lantern over the duke.

She leaned over to the dukes side and ripped open the shirt, "look John it's there"

"What is where?"

"The wound, look where the crossbow hit, she first pointed, then to Johns further disgust, poked her finger into the wound, causing puss and liquid to leak out. John covered his eyes,

"Madame please, this is desecration!" Mary looked up towards him,

"The wound John, it is minor, not deep enough to kill, I am no medical man but, I am sure this would not have killed him, wait there is something in the wound." Pushing another finger into the wound, John watched as she slowly pulled out a small black berry, she held it up to the light, then stood straight throwing the item away.

"Madame what is it?"

"It's a seed John, a plant seed. It is proof."

"Proof of what."

"If I am right John, it is a seed from a belladonna,"

"Madame I am confused,"

"Belladonna John, deadly nightshade, it is proof, the Duchess is right, the Duke was poisoned, murdered, but not by crossbow, but by poison. To get this in here, the person had to be close to him. One of the hunting party must have placed it into the wound," she paused, "to poison him, to kill him. To Johns relief, they returned to the lodgings, where Mary began pacing around the reception room,

"It was murder John, the Duchess was right, but who?"

"And why?" John replied. Mary paced around the room to John's annoyance, he was tired and had, in his eyes, spent the night desecrating a grave. Her pacing was wearing him and the floor thin.

"Madame!" he said, with possibly a little too much sharpness considering his position,

"If, the Duke was murdered, we must find out, who was in the hunting party and who tended to the duke after he was wounded, we need a full…" he paused for the word to come to him, "diary of the day and after."

Mary smiled at him,

"Yes john you are right, the first person to talk to is obvious."

"Madame, would you make it obvious to me,"

"The duchess,"

"But how do we gain access to her, privately, there are guards and that," he spat out the word, "Constable!"

Mary pondered for a minute then grinned and walked over to the table and picked up the bag of money the maid had left and weighed it in her palm,

"Well, the guards should be easy enough, as for the Constable, maybe he doesn't have to know about our visit." John was confused,

"Madame I do not understand?"

"There must be a servants entrance John, I doubt someone as self-important as the Constable would use it, but"

"But what?"

"Our new friend the maid would."

John and Mary walked in the morning drizzle towards the palace. Once inside their mood lifted, Mary in new britches and a new fresh shirt, courtesy of the Duchesses money, the same money saw the guard turn a blind eye and another escort them both up the tight wooden and creaky stairwell where the maid awaited them.

Madame Mary, Master John, welcome back to the palace. The duchess is expecting you.

As before they were taken into the grand reception room, but, this time by the servants entrance. Mary led the way and fell to her knees when close enough to the Duchess. The Duchess held out her hand which Mary accepted willingly.

"Madame, Duchess, so many thanks for the gift of the money, may the good Lord bless you. The Duchess leaned forward and stroked Marys new shirt collar.

"I see you have put it to good use, perhaps your friend John could also?" Mary turned to look at John, whose clothes were in need of a wash, or replacement.

Both woman began to laugh, John played his hat, then after noticing a hole, stopped.

"John," Mary began. "Perhaps you and Bravane could take a walk, together?"

Johns eyes widened, "Madame," he said moving to her, "We hardly know each other, is this appropriate?"

"John, my friend, are you shy? This would be a good chance to get to know her."

Soon, John and Bravane were outside the palace and walking together towards the river. Once there Bravane directed John towards the bridge, where once they were half-way to the other side, she stopped. Looking up at her tall escort, indicated with her hand towards the island in the river.

"This John is Ile Lacroix, my birthplace, my real home"

John was puzzled. "Do you not reside at the palace?"

"Yes" she replied but this little island is my true home, it is where I was raised, where I was loved and taught. Come" she said grabbing Johns' hand she led him down from the bridge onto the island.

"Bravane, "John exclaimed, "Where are you taking me?" John was unsure, he was in a strange town, indeed a strange country, but the touch of this fair young woman, caused a stirring in him, he dispelled it out of mind immediately, she was a fair and very pretty girl, but they were not betrothed. They should not have been touching.

John looked around, were people staring? At this older man with his young companion. Bravane had let go of his hand, but, no she held his arm as she guided him along the wooden slats which sat above the muddy street, towards their destination.

"Tell me Bravane, what am I looking at?" John stood as Bravane presented him with a view of an old blacksmith workshop. It was tidy and the smith was too busy working to notice them, but the building had definitely seen better days.

"It is my home" replied Bravane, well it was once, before..." her voice fell away into silence as she turned away from John.

"Before what? Please, I would like to know, you did bring me here to show me, there must be a reason Bravane."

Mary had entered the room, the Duchess was waiting for her, looking, in Marys eyes, as Regal as any queen she had ever met.

"Please," she said to Mary, before pausing "Madame, be seated. Mary wondered about the pause before Madame, sarcasm? Or an indication who was in charge, which, as she was paying for everything, she was.

"What have you found?"

"Duchess, Madame, you were right, your husband was murdered, but not by a crossbow."

The Duchess stared at her, her jewel like eyes seeming to bore inside her.

"Then how did he die, what have you discovered?" almost pleading, tears forming in her eyes

Mary had to think, She and John had opened his grave, without permission.

"My lady, you are not going to like this, but." Mary swallowed hard, she was in a corner now with no way out.

"John and I, John at my order we entered your husbands tomb." The duchess let out a gasp then composing herself grabbed Marys hand, tightly.

"Why, dear God why?" Mary turned from her, ashamed.

"My lady, we had to examine the body, to be sure, we found the wound, it was not deep, but something had been placed inside it."

"What, tell me I order you!" the Duchess was shouting now, her hand tightening around Marys, hurting her.

"We found a plant seed in the wound; it was Bella donna."

The Duchess face changed as she realised,

"Deadly Nightshade, he was murdered by one of the hunting party."

"It has to be, I'm so sorry."

The Duchess let go of Marys hand, then placed her hand on Marys face, gently.

"No, you have done what I asked. I will find who was on that hunting party.

The Duchess was gliding no longer, she was beyond fury as she entered the Constables' office, throwing the door open with so much force, all in the room, and indeed the room itself jumped in surprise.

"Constable! A word if you please!"

The constable tried to remain composed, but was shaken with this, he had never seen her so enflamed.

"Madame, how may I help you?"

All the Constables' staff began to back away, including his guards, partly out of respect of her position, but mostly out of fear.

The Duchess leaned over his desk placing her fists on the top.

"The hunting party, which led to my husbands," she paused, closed her eyes. "Murder"

The Constable looked around the room,

"Madame it was an accident, we have proof of an errand crossbow"

The Duchess grinned at him, "It was no accident, I have proof of the use of Belladonna, deadly nightshade"

"Proof, Madame, what proof?" he looked nervous and was beginning to sweat.

"Proof Constable that Belladonna was inserted into the crossbow wound to poison him, he was murdered, only someone close by could have done this, someone on that party, I want a list of names of those present and I want them now!"

The constables' hand shook as he wrote the list, then handed the paper over. The Duchess pacing the room, reading the list, then turned to the constable.

"Please ensure that none of these people leave the city," then she paused " including you."

With that she left the room as quickly as she had entered. Mary flooowing.

The constable dismissed his staff,

"Are you still there?"

"Yes constable" from behind the curtain Martell appeared. The constable opened his desk drawer, produced a bag of money. Then stood and walked over to chest, inserted a key and opened it. Producing a crossbow he walked over to Martell.

"This time, kill them both!"

Mary and John had received the list from the Duchess, via the maid, and were now walking through open parkland towards a clearing atop Mont Gargon, a hilltop overlooking the city. This was the spot where, according to the Duchess, the Duke was struck by a crossbow bolt which had deflected off a tree and struck him. Mary was not looking for the tree but a plant.

When she found it she called for John.

"Come, look, it's here." John strode over to her.

"What is here?"

Mary seemed to be proud of herself.

"Look John in there between those bushes, look, a green plant, this is what was used, I'm sure, this plant has foliage and berries are toxic" John looked but knew not what he was seeing.

"Madame, I do not understand, what am I looking for?"

"There John," she replied pointing, "Belladonna, Deadly nightshade, what really killed the Duke, I believe as the Duke was being treated for his wound, one of the party came over here, picked a berry and then inserted it into his wound. One of the party killed him, by poison."

"Who and why?"

"That is for us to discover. We will have to speak to everyone on the list, we must haste back to town to begin."

The pair turned, to be face with Martell with his now loaded crossbow.

"Quite the problem Mary, also, quite a problem, but not for me, I was sent here to kill you by my Edinburgh lord, now someone here wants you dead also, two people in different cities, countries want you dead, that is quite the feat. Still, one job and I get paid twice." He began laughing.

John stepped in between Martell and Mary,

"Mr Martell, you certainly have a problem you do not realise."

Martell stopped laughing,

"And what would that be?"

John withdrew the kitchen knife as Mary hid behind him.

"Your crossbow has one bolt and there are two of us. And we have a knife."

"You have a rusted blade, and I am close enough to fire this through both of you."

Realising this Mary took a sidestep as Martell raised the crossbow to shoulder height. Pointing it at Mary. John weighed his options, could he reach Martell before he fired for at this range the bolt would kill Mary.

Martell's face changed, then he fell forward a crossbow bolt deep in his back. Mary stared then almost shouted at John.

"Where did that come from, fired by who?"

"Madame look?" A small figure could be seen through the trees running away.

John looked at Mary,

"Should I give chase?"

"No John, let us get home, quickly"

Mary, returning to male attire, with John visited all those on the list, all held their story, the Duke was felled by an errant crossbow bolt, which had rebounded off a tree and impaled him. Mary was convinced this was a pre-arranged story as all those questioned gave the same answers to her questions.

John, speaking little French listened on as Mary quizzed the party members in French, returning to the house by the cathedral, Mary explained her suspicions.

John thought on this,

"If they are all plotting together, who are they trying to protect and why?"

"John" Mary responded, "If they are all together and hiding the truth, it must be someone very powerful or very rich, or both. Who in this group holds that type of power?"

John and Mary stared at each other as they both realized,

"The Constable!" they said in unison.

"It must be him," John continued, he is rich enough and has the power of the entire Duchy, now the Duke is gone, Madame, I am only guessing but, with the Duke dead, he would become the Duke in all but name, would he not?"

Mary considered this,

"Yes John he would, but we can't simply accuse him, we have no concrete proof, as for bribing those people, It would take a lot of cash, how much money would he need?"

"The Constable is vastly wealthy; he has been using his position to advance his finances for years."

Mary looked quizzical, "In what way?"

"I am told madame," he paused, "If the parents of a family die, he takes over their estate, on behalf of the town, officially until any child is of age, then he sends the children away, and while they are away, gone, sells all they have. And keeps the money for himself."

"John," Mary stared at him, "How do you know this?"

"Bravane told me. She was one of his victims, her father was a Blacksmith, after her parents died, he took hold of their shop and sent her away to England."

"How could Bravane tell you this? You do not speak French." Mary replied, then realisation befell her .

"She told you in English?" John nodded his reply, Mary continued "How does a mere Maid a Blacksmiths daughter, speak English, she would not be educated."

John, unhappy with Bravane being called mere, knew his place and held silence Mary continued her train of thought.

"Unless she had spent time in England, which would prove her story. Come John I wish to revisit Gargon, the site where the Duke was shot by the crossbow, how could a crossbow bolt rebound of a tree, surely it would stick in the wood?"

Mary was pacing around the clearing; John was watching for another possible attack. Mary stopped and patted a large tree.

"This is the tree John, the one which rebounded the bolt into the Duke."

John walked over to her and noticed something, he started to run his fingers over the section of bark.

"Madame," he said, "Look at this, this section of bark has been cut, look!"

Mary peered; he was right there appeared to be a thin gash in the outer layer of the wood.

"John your knife please," He handed over the kitchen knife, it was old and blunt but with enough effort between them they managed to get the piece of bark out.

"Look John, here" Mary said handing him the piece.

"What am I looking at madame?"

"The edge John, look how smooth it is, like it has been cut deliberately with a knife or a saw."

John began to think aloud, "Madame you said how could a crossbow bolt rebound of a tree, what if something was placed behind the bark to make it bounce, something metallic."

"But who could make such a thing, only a blacksmith."

John stared at Mary, "Or a blacksmiths daughter, I think we should go and speak with Bravane."

Mary raised her hand to stop him, "Wait John, why would she want to kill the Duke?"

"That, Madame, will be our first question."

It was getting dark by the time the two gentlemen of Edinburgh walked through the crampt cobbled streets of Rouen towards to the Ducal palace.

Mary itched in the evening heat, her shirt was male and rougher than she was accustomed to. Years of fine clothing had not prepared her for these cheaper harder wearing clothing.

As they stood at the servant's entrance, John looked at her,

"Are you alright Madame?" his concern genuine. Mary smiled,

"Sorry John, this is silly of me, I am used to finer, more," she paused and laughed, "Ladylike attire."

John laughed also, "I had never considered this madame. Forgive me."

"For what exactly, I bought these garments myself, but I will forgive you for calling me Madame, if you stop and revert to James."

"Yes Mad," stopping himself, "James"

The door opened, two armed guards stood before them, Mary quickly and quietly conversed with them in French, John stood in silence understanding little, but knew when to hand over the coins for entry.

The two were led through the bare narrow corridors of the servant area, a true contrast to the opulence of the Ducal rooms, a short while later in one of these lavish rooms, they found Bravane.

"Good sirs, I am instructed you wish to see me, may I enquire as to why?" she spoke softly, quietly as she bowed gently to them. Her English flawless.

Mary spoke first,

"I believe I, well, both John and I, owe you a large debt of gratitude?"

Bravane looked confused,

"I am afraid I do not understand, is this a trick?"

Mary walked over to her,

Mont Gargan, in the clearing, it was you with the crossbow, was it not." Bravane looked toward the floor, her demeaner confirming to Mary her guilt,

"Please, sirs, I felt I had no choice, he was set to kill you both."

Mary took her hand and led her to a couch,

"This is true, Martell was ready to kill us, but you stopped him and saved us, but why?"

Bravane, holding back her tears,

"Because I need you," pausing to compose herself, "Pleas sirs," looking directly at Mary,

"Madame, forgive me, I have been, as you say eavesdropping, there are many hidden places within this palace, where I can hear, conversations." Mary smiled at her.

"So, you have been listening to my, conversations with your mistress, I should be upset but I know, servants do this everywhere."

"Also, Madame," John interjected, "without this, we would most likely be dead."

"True John, true." Turning back to Bravane, "You still have not answered my question, why?"

"I overheard you with my Mistress, how you had examined the Dukes body and found proof of poison. I was so relieved" She began to sob, "I thought I had killed him, I never meant to hurt him I swear, I meant no harm to him."

Mary looked at John, both looked confused.

"If you meant no harm to the duke, then who was the crossbow bolt for?"

Bravane breathed heavily, then looking at the floor began to sob as she confessed.

"The constable madame, he is an odious man, he is plotting against the duchess, I know it, you see Madame, years ago, I lived with my parents on the isle known as (Name), I showed you John, do you remember?" She looked at him, he nodded, her sense of relief obvious.

"Then my family died, I was removed by the constable, he wanted the shop and the home for his people, my home, it should be mine, he sent me away, to England to friends of his, they abused me, I escaped and returned under a false name, I managed to gain employment here in an attempt of revenge, I wanted to kill him for what he had done, I forged the metal, I hid it in the tree to deflect the arrow towards him.
It would appear to all it flew from the North, his party would look there, allowing me to flee South, but the Duke moved in the way, it was too late, I had already fired, it hit him, I swear Madame, it was not meant for him, it was meant for the constable, he has to be stopped."

"Why?" Mary enquired.

"Because" she replied, "He is one of them"

"One of whom"

"Huguenot. He is taking properties across the city, and giving them to his Hugunot friends, when there are enough, they will rise up and take over, the Duchess is in grave danger, he has to be stopped, this is why I helped you, she will believe you, no-one will believe a mere maid.

Mary had decided, John could tell but the look in her eyes, she would not be stopped, as she walked briskly, almost running, toward the Constables chambers, she did not wait for an invite or introduction. She pushed the doors open, surprising the guards and infuriating the Constable.

"How dare you Madame! Enter here without invite or permission!"

Mary calmed herself,

"Are you, or are you not a Huguenot?"

The constable approached her, John, catching up stood behind her waiting to be called.

"What is the meaning of this, woman!"

"Please answer the question, are you or are you not, a Huguenot?"

The constable stared directly at her,

"And what business is that of you Madame."

Mary grinned, then after John was by her side spoke slowly.

"It has come to my attention, Sir, that you have been possessing the homes and businesses of trades people all over this city."

"Madame, I have in the name of the Dukedom, on behalf of the Duke."

"Who you murdered on the hunting trip, with hemlock."

The constable laughed,

"Madame, my dear lady, the Duke, God bless him was killed by an assassin, hiding in the woods, a crossbow bolt deflected from a tree and impaled him, there were witnesses, speak with them they will confirm."

"I have sir, they all confirm your story, but were you not the one to attend to the Duke, you alone sir, was it not you who had the opportunity to insert the deadly nightshade, the Hemlock poison, into the wound causing death, the crossbow bolt, did not impale the Duke deeply enough to cause death."

The constable leant on his desk,

"And how exactly would you know this Madame,"

Quickly, her temper rising, Mary replied, "Because sir, I have examined the wound Sir."

"You were in his tomb, desercrating his body, God forgive, I will see you hang my Lady."

"The only one to see a noose will be you sir, you conspired to bring Hugunotes into this city, with the intention of taking over and making yourself the Duke. All those on the hunting party, they were all Huguenot friends of yours, in your pocket, aware of the plan, rid the town of the Duke and take over, but an assassin, an attempt to kill you failed, but you saw an opportunity and you took it. Is that not true sir."

The Constable laughed,

"My Lady Seton, yes, I am a Huguenot, Yes I wanted the Duke out of the way and yes I took my opportunity, well done, for a mere woman you are rather intelligent, but who will believe the word of a foreign woman over mine?"

"No-one but they will believe mine," All fell silent as the Duchess entered the room,

"Constable, you killed my husband in cold blood, I will see you hang for this, Guards!"

The guards filled the room, and soon were dragging the resisting constable away. Mary bowed the duchess, then spoke,

"My Lady, how did you hear?"

The duchess began to laugh,

"My good Lady Seton, Bravane is not the only one who knows where to hide in this palace, to overhear private conversations."

"My lady, I have been to Paris, but to no avail,"

Mary was despondent, "Will the King not help?"

The duchess took Marys hand "He would have but it is too late."

Mary face was ashen, "Duchess she is not dead?"

"No but she is under arrest, by order of the Tudor."

John and Mary returned to their lodgings with another reward from the Duchess, upon arrival John insisted on returning home.

"I do not think it is possible John, it would not be safe, Bothwell would have us killed."

Then there was a knock on the door, a man entered, speaking in French to Mary, he leaves.

Mary tells John of his suspicion of his brother's death.

Mary smiled to herself,

"John, it would appear that news of us and the duke's death has travelled quickly in this town. He wishes us to find out the truth regarding his brothers' accident."

John smiled to himself, "So we are not to return, just yet."

THE END